STRETCH TO CONNECT

FINDING BALANCE AND HARMONY WITH YOUR HORSE

PAULA CURTIS

Disclaimer of Liability

Paula Curtis, Because Of The Horse and Jack and Paula Curtis LLC, shall have neither liability nor responsibility to any person, horse or entity with respect to any harm, loss or damage caused or alleged to be caused directly or indirectly by the information and exercises contained in this book.

BECAUSE OF
THE HORSE
PUBLISHING

Stretch To Connect

Finding Balance and Harmony With Your Horse

ISBN: 978-0-578-50282-3

For all inquiries, including clinic scheduling

contact Office@jackandpaulacurtis.com

For Inspiration Visit The YouTube Channel: Jack And Paula Curtis Horsemanship

DEDICATION

This book is dedicated to all the heart-centered, horse-centered horse owners out there. Students of the horse who are truly dedicated to their horses' well-being, willingly and eagerly look for information to help them on their quest to be better stewards to their horses. Together we can impact the equestrian community in a positive way, helping horses and humans alike, finding methods that promote kindness, fairness, and regard for all living beings.

To my two children, Claire and Jackson Curtis, Your kindness and fun-and-loving energy is the thing that makes you both so special, never let the world take that from you.

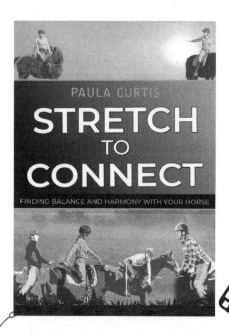

DOWNLOAD A FREE TRAINING ON THE STRETCHES IN THIS BOOK!

Just to say thanks for buying my book, I would like to give you a free training related to the stretches in this book. Including...

- Free Video
- Free, Coach On Your Shoulder Audio Lessons
- Free PDF

TO DOWNLOAD GO TO:
https://www.jackandpaulacurtis.com/pl/76343

CONTENTS

ACKNOWLEDGMENTS

To my husband Jack Curtis. Your love and support has been there since the beginning, through most anything life can bring, allowing me to pursue my dreams wholeheartedly. You push me to have confidence and self-assurance that most certainly has led me to write this book. Our quest for better horsemanship has been a journey we have pursued together since the beginning of us. You've led me to so many discoveries and understandings about human nature and the nature of the horse that otherwise would have gone unnoticed.

Also, my parents, Don and Rosanne Korinek. You've exposed me to world-class horsemen and horsemanship since very early on. Since the beginning you have believed in me and offered me opportunities that put me on the path I am on right now, always guiding me to opportunity and growth. Mom—you've always helped me be clearer and more concise in my writing and although in my school years I did not appreciate it, now I do!

To all the horses who have passed through my life for the many lessons you have afforded me. Your patience guides me in the things I need to know, yet fumble through, always forgiving and kind. You have been great teachers and mirrors, allowing me to learn the lessons that truly matter.

To all the teachers and clinicians with whom I have ridden and watched, I am a sponge, and feel I am merely teaching what you and my horses have taught me. Your inspiration has no beginning or end. It just permeates my being, and I am so grateful for that.

I would also like to acknowledge these people, in no particular order.

Jeff and Rosie Curtis, Sue Lorenz, Lois Korinek, Gertrude Lorenz, Lee Smith, Mary Beaumier, and All of my past Students, for their guidance, inspiration, and support.

INTRODUCTION

Y ou must first work on yourself if you want improvement in your horse.

Inspired by that truth, and all the experiences that led me to it, this book is a culmination of thousands of lessons taken and taught since 1994, of hundreds of clinics and horse shows and seminars. I have coached riders up to national titles in a variety of disciplines, including dressage, gymkhana events, hunter/jumpers, western dressage, etc. Through it all, I always knew that my goal was an ever greater connection with the horses and riders I worked with, and that the key laid in stretching myself, emotionally, mentally, physically.

Paula Showing her Appaloosa FEI Prix St. George level.

I grew up on a horse farm where my parents board-ed horses, offered lessons, and trained. Horses have been a part of my life since birth. My parents regularly had clinicians at the farm who promoted excellence in horsemanship, exposing me to these theories through feel and understanding of the horse. Being on the farm afforded me the opportunity to apply the techniques I learned from them on a wide variety of horses. By the age of fifteen, I was teaching horsemanship and training horses. It has been my one and only career.

Paula Jumping Bridleless. Photo by Sally Moskol.

The road has not always been an easy one. At the age of four, I was diagnosed with juvenile rheumatoid arthritis. With horses, I found a way to be athletic and equal to my peers, even if my body wasn't that of a normal child, but instead closer to an arthritic sixty-year-old. I had swollen, painful joints in my knees, hips, feet, elbows, and hands. But I had horses, and they gave me wings. I jumped, I galloped, I barrel raced, I did dressage. Because of the horse, I could do more and be more.

Although I loved gymkhana, western saddles hurt my knees and hips, so I just rode in my English saddle. At the age of sixteen, I qualified and competed at the NBHA World championships, the only one of 2000 competitors in an English saddle. This way of riding taught me the importance of having a centered, balanced seat.

Paula at NBHA World Championships, notice the English saddle,
the only one of over 2000 competitors to do so.

At the age of 16, I began dating my now-husband. Since we were both teaching horsemanship and training horses, we did some of our work together. We were, and continue to be, a great team, pushing each other to learn more, to be students of—and advocates for—the horse.

Because of my arthritis, I was a regular at Milwaukee Children's Hospital. Through some great physical therapists, I was exposed to the benefits of stretching, regular exercise, and the idea of move it or lose it. Very early on, I learned the importance of functional movement patterns and the necessity of finding the movements that work best for you.

Then, in my mid-thirties, I was out on the trails at our farm, riding a young warmblood mare I had recently started. Though she had only a handful of rides under saddle, she behaved perfectly until we were almost home when she inexplicably began bucking. I decided to do an emergency dismount, but unfortunately I kept hold of the inside rein and—with her still bucking and unbalanced—I ended up pulling her on top of me.

The results were predictable. Multiple injuries, mostly to my ribcage and shoulders, required several surgeries and metal plates in my ribcage to get every thing back in order.

My experiences dealing with arthritis spurred me to begin stretching almost immediately after the accident and, by the time I began physical therapy, I was ahead of schedule. However, my left latissimus dorsi (the broadest muscle of the back, running from the middle to the lower back), was not firing or activating. Fortunately for me, Dr. Daniel J Kristl, DPT, PT, OCS, CMT an amazing physical therapist, was there to help. I was intrigued by the therapy process and asked Dan questions. He happily explained the inner workings of the body and what we were doing to help create functional movement again. After therapy, I would go home and pour over literature about the shoulder and torso muscles and how the body worked together in movement. I became aware of the fascia and marveled at just how interconnected the entire body is. Previously, physical therapy had addressed my limbs and arthritic joints; this new physical therapy was fascinating because I had not had to deal with torso and shoulder problems before.

It is one thing to read about these challenges and another to live them. When you actually have to apply the knowledge to your own body, the depth of learning that occurs is incredible. This horrible situation turned into a profound learning experience for me. The things I learned then, I use each and every time I work with my students, helping them find a better position and fix riding problems.

Believe it or not, I am grateful for my arthritis and injuries because they have given me many tools as a rider and teacher, providing insights into my students and how I can help them. Once I applied the power of stretching to my teaching, helping my students explore their range of movement as they rode, they became better riders, and connected with their horses as if by magic. Voila! By working on themselves—shaping, improving, advancing—they shaped and improved and advanced their horses.

Paula Eventing

HELPING
HORSES
AND PEOPLE

Find inner harmony so you can find harmony with your horse. Harmony between the horse and rider is the greatest success!

Finding harmony with your horse is such a wonderful thing, and it has always been something I strive for in my riding, and the focus of my teaching. If we seek harmony, we will find it, so it is important to go looking for it. Sometimes we need to completely shift the way we approach a ride to access the harmony we are seeking.

Helping horses and their people in a meaningful way has forever been my focus, and a book seemed the next logical step. Because of my love for the horse and my desire to help people understand their horses, incorporating stretching is a part of my own and my students' workouts.

Early on, it was apparent to me that riders came to their lessons in a state that had no part in the horse's world— uptight, tense, distracted, etc. This has gotten worse over the years as we get ever more distracted by all of the "gadgets" in our lives.

Instead of the barn being a sanctuary, it is just another place where your anxieties—work, school, e-mails, texts, etc.—can follow you. This is not good for you, and not good for the horse.

I've gotten frustrated with students who are not helping their horses. I have always taught for the benefit of these wonderful animals. It is my life's purpose. I've been hard on my students, encouraging them to make changes. Oftentimes they do, but sometimes they do not. Not because they do not want to, but because they cannot. Dialing into the root of this, what I have found includes held breath, a distracted mind, agitation from inner stress, lack of awareness, body tension, immobility, fear, thinking but not feeling—the list goes on and on.

In order to help the horse, I realized I first had to help the person. I had to help the rider be present, aware, and connected, to slow down and drop into this very moment. If I could do that, then I could help many more horses and their humans.

For riders, being present has become increasingly difficult. They carry all of the pressures of the world around with them. Because of this, they come to the barn stressed, their senses overloaded, their minds on too many things, yet nothing at all. *Remember, there is a direct correlation between mind, body and spirit.*

Is this you? Stress and electronics leaving you in a hunched over posture?

Horses live in the moment; their lives are slow-paced, and they don't wear wrist watches.

When we enter their lives rushed and carrying tension, the horse does not understand how to react to it. When you do the stretches outlined in this book notice the huge changes you see in your horse as he relaxes and realizes you are making a mental shift. He may yawn, lower his head, lick and chew, move more freely. Horses make great mirrors, oftentimes reflecting back to us our mental state.

We all have heard that we need to change ourselves if we want to change our horses.

YOU HOLD A SIMPLE KEY TO PROFOUND CHANGE.

While experimenting with these exercises, you will notice that the shackles the world puts on you begin to melt away as you connect with the "here and now". Doing the exercises not only loosens and stretches those tight areas, but you will find an internal connection and relaxation that lays the foundation for a great ride.

Get rid of stress, tension and fear. Stretch!
Through the stretches outlined in this book you will find a way to get rid of the stress, tension, and fear you may carry. Allowing you to connect with your horse in a way that is meaningful to both of you.

THE HORSE

The horse is always operating from his perspective; it is your job to see it. Feel of, and for, your horse with your heart.

Wyhen you get into the zone with your horse, it becomes much easier to see things from your horse's perspective. When you see things his way, your training becomes much more effective. When riding, or anytime we are with our horses for that matter, we are in a conversation with them. A conversation goes two ways. By seeing the horse's point of view it allows us to adjust our approach as necessary to better explain our ideas.

The horse appreciates the rider slowing down, relaxing, breathing—in other words, entering a space where they can connect from the heart. This is the space that generates true appreciation from both horse and human. When humans open their hearts and really feel, there is a huge shift in the relationship they have with their horses.

Horses then communicate from that same space because they understand it. They mirror what we offer. The humans' intentions then become clear to the horse.

Reciprocity occurs between horse and human, both giving and appreciating one another, each grateful for what the other brings into their world.

I aim for the shift from thinking to feeling, from being in a space where stress and agitation lie, to one in which gratitude, love and appreciation rule. A state of flow evolves, a feeling of being in the zone.

The best part is that stretching is simple! We can all do it without having to overthink, making stretching on horseback a truly wonderful tool. As we explore each stretch, the horse's movement encourages our bodies to let go. It moves us through a variety of planes, allowing us to stretch farther and in different ways than stretching on solid ground would do. Therapeutic riding has known this for years—time for the rest of us to incorporate it into our everyday rides.

The answer to improved riding, to an improved relationship with the horse, lies in a simple stretch! Who would have thought that something as basic as stretching could offer such profound change? But it does!

BENEFITS OF STRETCHING

Practice self-discipline versus horse discipline.

As riders, we always strive to be better. We work on countless things, such as training exercises, body position, timing and application of the aids, understanding the horse's mind, etc. Stretching on horseback helps us achieve all these goals and it creates great riders.

Why? Let's look at some of the reasons:

FUN AND IMPROVES RIDING FOR ANY DISCIPLINE!

Have fun and improve your riding, stretch!

You ride to explore, question, and try new things. It is not a serious matter; you do not need to adhere to a perfect form, since you are experimenting and moving through a range of motion. It takes the pressure off both you and your horse. Research shows that you learn much faster if you are having fun while you learn.

A FEAR REDUCER!

Find inner stillness, relax, becoming present and in the moment.

Stretching can help fearful riders become more confident. Stretching makes riders purposefully end up in positions that might not feel natural, so they learn that, even though they feel out of control, the body still has the balance and ability to stabilize. This is a big relief! As a rider, you can manage the horse's movement and have mastery of your body at the same time. It feels great to know this, not just in your mind, but also in your body, specifically your reflexes. Stretching encourages breathing, which encourages relaxation and confidence, banishing the fear that saps your enjoyment of riding and your ability to ride well.

CONNECTS YOU
WITH YOUR HORSE

*Stretching helps you get good at going with, and
blending with, your horse before you direct him.*

The connection with my horse is my favorite benefit of stretching on horseback. By shifting our intentions and focusing on ourselves, we take the pressure to perform off the horse. We have all heard that horses know how to be horses; we know that it is us, the riders, who need to change. Well, stretching facilitates that change! When we stretch, we find an inner stillness. We let the stress and tension of the day melt away, becoming quieter, and therefore better at listening to our horses. We become quiet observers. We watch our horses' responses; we enter into a conversation. Because we slow down, we let go of anxiety, our heart rate slows, and we breathe deeply and easily. We are present and in the moment. These are all important to our horses. Horses are incredibly perceptive—they feel this shift in us—and you will see them relax, become supple, and tune in because of it. This sets the stage for a successful ride.

*You cannot take out of a horse what
you do not give him first.*

ENCOURAGES THE POWER
OF EXPERIMENTATION

Experimentation gives you permission to make mistakes. Mistakes are an opportunity for learning.

When we focus too much on the perfect textbook position, we can become rigid. We contort our bodies to the so-called ideal and, in the process, lock up various muscles and joints. This removes us from the thinking-feeling state necessary to connect with our bodies and with our horses in meaningful ways. Our horses respond with tension, reflecting back to us what we ourselves are doing. Alternately, when we stretch, we create new patterns of movement that helps us more naturally find perfect positions.

Experimenting with different patterns opens new neural pathways, enabling you to be comfortable in a wide variety of positions on horseback. It creates a safe space to allow your body to learn and be okay with being out of position. You break ingrained bad habits and patterns of movement, replacing them with new and more functional movements. You become more pliable, easily adapting if things go wrong: the horse spooks or bolts, you get jumped out of position, etc. Your body relaxes even in awkward positions because it intuitively knows how to orchestrate itself to remain in balance.

In some of the stretches I teach, you will play around with riding extremes in your range of motion and then find the neutral position for yourself. This increases awareness, beneficial when you are trying to find a better position, changing horses, saddles, etc.

IMPROVES MULTITASKING

Independent aids allow clear and accurate communication.

As riders, we need to be able to do many things in a given moment. Stretching helps with that as it teaches us to be able to execute a multitude of movements, all while reading the horses' responses, while steering, while being aware of our environment. This facilitates independence of the aids, so we can clearly and accurately communicate to our horses.

IMPROVES AWARENESS

Get to know your inner dialogue; let stretching help you become aware of it; this awareness can create great change.

Awareness affords us the ability to make changes, notice what those changes do, and make more changes accordingly. These ridden exercises are slow and purposeful, giving us permission to be aware and drop into the moment, noticing the important things.

We must be mindful of our own mental state and the state of our horses. Stretching on horseback creates a space for us to check in to both our own and our horses' emotions, as we unwind from our day and work toward relaxing and becoming available to one another. We become conscious of areas where we may be holding tension, enabling us to release the area. We become aware of the here and now, which is the moment that matters most to us and our horses.

IMPROVES OBSERVATION

"Observe, Remember, Compare." ~Alexander Graham Bell

Through awareness, you increase your power of observation, allowing you to be more objective in the way you see things. When you do these exercises, it can be very helpful to make these observations and record them. You can then quantify your successes and celebrate them. You may find it helpful to train your eye by taking "before" and "after" pictures. Anything that sharpens your perceptions will be invaluable to you and to your horse.

Be your own teacher.

IMPROVES BREATHING

Better breathing helps connect body and mind.

Stretching brings about better breathing. You breathe deeper and more fully; as you let go of tension, you yawn. Focus on breathing into the stretches and then breathing the tension out. Soon the power of focused breathing will be apparent, and you will naturally want to incorporate it into the rest of your ride.

BEFORE MOVING ON

The horse invites us to be our best selves.

... Consider These Helpful Ideas:

SOFT EYES

This is something you can practice both off and on the horse. When you look ahead—whether you are riding, walking, jogging, bicycling, driving, etc.—make sure to keep your peripheral vision open. Instead of focusing on one thing right in front of you, let yourself see the whole picture, both up and down and to the sides. Then you can take in the environment as your horse does, aware of all that is going on around you, not just what is directly in front of you.

QUESTIONING AND VISUALIZATIONS

After each exercise, I will ask a few questions. My goal is to keep you open to possibilities and self-discovery. If I tell you the so-called "correct" answers, you may not find your answer. I have learned so much from my students over the years by asking them questions and helping them interpret their answers. I will do the same for you. I will also give you visualizations to help guide you and keep you in a "feeling" state. Since a picture is worth a thousand words, visualizations provide the mental imagery you can recall time and time again.

BODY SCANNING

Before and after each stretch, employ a brief body scan so you recognize the changes that occur in the stretch. Be aware of your muscle tone when doing the scan, noting areas where muscles are working hard or are not working at all. You may find it helpful to keep a record, jotting down the changes you notice in yourself and your horse.

LISTENING TO YOUR HORSE

I will regularly encourage you to watch and feel your horse to discover what he is telling you. Your horse has a lot to say, although he says it through body language. This means that you are going to read that body language, the eyes, ears, nostrils, muscle tone, etc. As you move through a variety of stretches, reading the changes in your horse as you do them will become much easier. If you do a stretch and your horse is uncomfortable, find out why. Maybe your saddle moves in a way that is painful during that stretch. Or perhaps you grip with your leg as you do the stretch. Try to find out what causes the horse's discomfort and remove that unpleasant stimulus. Listen to your horse!

REACTING TO PAIN RESPONSIBLY

Pain is an indicator that tells you when to stop. If you feel pain while doing any of the exercises, please stop. Do not push the stretch too far. Skip a painful exercise altogether if it consistently pushes you across the pain threshold. Some discomfort may be okay, but please be aware of your body's limitations.

When stretching, it is important to not overdo yet to do enough to reap the benefits. As with many things there is a sweet spot, and you will need to find your own. To begin, I recommend holding the stretches for approximately thirty seconds and then build from there. Stretching while horseback is quite dynamic, and therefore you will feel the horse's natural movement create mini-stretches with each stride.

KEEPING YOUR SADDLE LEVEL

The level saddle is a very important platform for effectively doing your stretches. If your saddle is not level, that will affect your riding in various ways. The brain's primary job is to keep you alive—and for that you need to be balanced. If your brain senses imbalance, you will not be able to fully relax. If your saddle is tipped either up or down, your brain knows that the ground you "stand on" is not stable; muscles will then hold tension, striving to put you in positions that keep your brain the safest. This will cause undesirable postural adjustments. Do yourself a favor and make sure your saddle is level. If you would like to dive deeper into this subject, we offer a mini-course on saddle fit and achieving a level saddle.

PACING YOURSELF

Safety First! Initially, do the stretches at a standstill, especially if you feel unsure of your abilities or how your horse may react. Most benefits typically occur at the walk since that gait rocks us softly as we stretch. You may also do many exercises at the trot and canter, but use your own good judgment or seek the guidance of a professional. A coach or trainer will be able to help you determine if you or your horse are prepared enough to do the exercises at greater speed. I also have an online course on these exercises and more, which can help you determine at what level and speed you should be doing these stretches.

STARTING WISELY

When you begin, pick a stretch or two and experiment with only those for a couple of rides before attempting additional stretches. Feel the benefits each stretch offers by really focusing on the stretch and doing it slowly and purposefully. You will find you gravitate toward particular stretches, and that is perfectly fine. As you play around with these, key into the stretches that do the most for both you and your horse. These are the stretches you will revisit frequently. You may also find tight areas that you need to focus on out of the saddle as well. Great!

Sections are organized by "general area", although you will feel the waves of any one stretch ripple through the rest of your body.

When stretching, it is important to not overdo, yet to do enough to reap the benefits. As with many things, there is a sweet spot, and you will need to find your own. To begin, I recommend holding the stretches for approximately thirty seconds and then build from there. Stretching while horseback is quite dynamic, and therefore you will feel the horse's natural movement create mini-stretches with each stride.

YOUR BEST SEAT

THE SEAT IS THE FOUNDATION OF OUR BALANCE WHEN WE RIDE.

W e will begin with exercises that will help you find your best seat, the one in which you can allow the horse's movement to go through you in a free-flowing manner, the one in which you feel stable, secure, and pain-free. Over the many years I have been teaching, I have realized that what works for one person may not work for another—and that is okay! We all have different conformation, injuries, ailments, etc. Certain positions and stretches that are very helpful for one person may not be helpful for another.

Through experimentation and questioning, we are going to find your ideal position.

The job of the seat is to receive the horse's movement in the way that creates balance and the least amount of interference with the horse's back. This makes it easier on both rider and horse. When the seat is in this neutral position, the rest of the rider's body can move freely and the brain knows everything is okay because the rider is balanced. Overall, for both body and mind, tension is relieved.

How do you find that, you may ask? You begin by experimenting with riding the extremes, becoming aware of how they affect your ride. When riding the extremes, you fully explore your range of motion by opening and closing your angles to the end of their range of motion. You stretch yourself in one direction and then another, moving between the two to find the middle position in which you can be most effective, comfortable, and elegant.

I would encourage you to do the following brief check of your seat at the beginning of each ride, creating the base of support that allows you to maximize your stretches.

Begin by walking on your horse around the arena. Notice the contact points in the saddle.

Ask:

- How does the movement go through me?

- Is it blocked anywhere?

- Do I feel any tension or bracing?

- What contact points do I notice in my seat, thigh, and lower leg?

NOW. Let's experiment.

EXERCISE ONE: ROCK THE CHAIR

· ◦ — ◉ — ◦ ·

Summary of Steps:

- Begin at a standstill, sitting quietly on your horse. sit on the back side of your seat bones, (the back of your "rocking chair", as you might visualize the seat bones) stretching your lower back, looking at your bellybutton to increase the stretch.

- Sit on the front of your seat bones, (the front of your "rocking chair" rockers) hollowing your back, lifting your ribcage and stretching the front of your body.

- Move between the two until you find your middle/ neutral seat.

- When you are comfortable try this exercise at the various gaits; walk, trot, and canter.

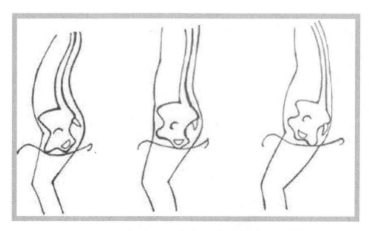

The range of motion of the pelvis in the saddle.

ROCK THE CHAIR - THE STEPS IN DETAIL

STEP 1:

Put your seat in a position where the front of your pelvis (your pubic bone) is lifted, and you are sitting on the back of your seat bones. You can use your lower abdominal muscles to help lift the front of your pelvis up.

Ask:

- What does this do to the feeling of my horse's movement, both in my seat and in the rest of my body?

- How does my horse's movement move through me?

- Does the movement get blocked anywhere?

- How does my lower back grow out of my seat?

- How does it change the contact of my thigh against the saddle? My knee?

- What does my horse tell me about this position? Watch the horse's eyes and ears, noticing muscle tone as well.

STEP 2:

Repeat the experiment but this time ride on the front upturned edges of your seat-bones and your pubic bone, asking yourself the same questions.

Observe:

While doing these exaggerated movements, you may have noticed your thighs move away from the saddle (when you are on the back of your seat-bones) or you may have pinched your knees (when you were on the front end of your seat-bones and pubic bone).

Also, your lower back will either flatten or hollow. You may have noticed your horse's movement did not pass freely through your body when riding these extremes.

Already you are making observations and becoming more aware—this is what separates good riders from great ones! Pat yourself on the back! You are practicing a skill that all great riders have, a skill you will continue to develop.

STEP 3:

Play around with the two extremes, both on the front of the pelvis, (hollow back) position and the rolled under (flattened back) position. Find the one in the middle where you feel a nice stable seat platform that allows the movement to pass through your body easily without restriction. It should be a middle/neutral seat. If you think about your two seat bones, the neutral position will be the one in which the seat bones point straight down.

STEP 4:

When you are comfortable at the walk, ride the extremes at various gaits and continue to build your awareness and ask questions.

Ask:

Does the position facilitate:

- Good connection along the entirety of the leg?

- A platform on which to stack the rest of my body?

- An allowing of the horse's movement to pass

through me?

- The least amount of effort to remain balanced and in control?

- A soft back with a neutral spine?

Visualize:

- Your seat (pelvis, buttocks, etc.) is like a rocking chair.

- Riding the waves passing through it.

- Heavy and tired, like a sleeping child.

- Weighted yet supple (I use this idea when communicating to the horse to be quiet or while slowing down).

- Like a tripod, stable.

- A bubbling pot of water (I use this idea to communicate to the horse to have energy).

- The seat invites the horse's back up into it.

- Open and wide seat, it surrounds the saddle/back.

- Flashlights on your seat bones point straight down.

IN CONCLUSION:

Look for your pelvis to be in the middle of its range of movement. This is only a starting point; you may not have your perfect seat quite yet. What you do have is a greater awareness of the seat, its options, and what position or positions seem to feel—and work—best for you and your horse. As you stretch and grow more flexible and aware in the saddle, you will find your seat improves even further. The whole body is connected and interrelated so working on each piece will have a ripple effect through the rest of the body.

A STRONG AND SUPPLE MIDDLE

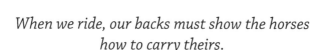

When we ride, our backs must show the horses how to carry theirs.

Horses do a great job of reflecting our posture in theirs. Therefore, we must be aware of how we hold our backs as this will affect how the horses holds theirs.

Once your pelvis is in a neutral position, the next logical thing to talk about is the torso and back. Think of your back growing out of the pelvis, strong and supple. When the spine is in its middle range of motion, the small curves act as shock absorbers. Unfortunately, many spines do not have a nice soft curve; instead, they have an exaggerated curve—either hollow or rounded/hunched—where the spine is unable to move any farther in that particular direction. This creates compression on one side and tension on the other. The goal is to have a mobile, flexible spine in the middle of its range of motion. It will then absorb movement from any direction.

When you first start stretching on horseback, your horse may wonder what you are doing and be a little unsure or insecure. Begin at a halt with this exercise to get the horse comfortable with you moving in new and various positions. In turn this will create relaxation in both you and your horse, setting the stage to do it in forward motion.

EXERCISE TWO: STRETCH THE BACK AND CONNECT WITH THE HORSE

Summary of Steps:

- Beginning at a halt, reach your right hand across the withers and scratch your horse on the left shoulder, reaching farther down to increase the stretch.

- Reach your right hand back and scratch the right side of your horse on the hindquarters.

- Switch hands and repeat on the other side.

- When you are comfortable you can proceed to do this stretch in forward motion.

Keep your saddle centered, and your seat over your feet as you rub down the horse's shoulder.

STRETCH THE BACK AND CONNECT WITH THE HORSE - THE STEPS IN DETAIL

STEP 1:

Begin at the halt. Once your horse is comfortable, you can continue at the walk. Reach your right hand across the withers, rubbing your way down the horse's left shoulder. Begin at the withers and gradually deepen the stretch as you scratch or rub your way down the shoulder. Always watch your horse to see his reaction, stopping at spots he enjoys being rubbed.

Be aware of the stretch along your back and ribs. Feel and move into the stretch, opening and lengthening your back. Increase the stretch by breathing more fully into your lung on the side you are stretching. Think of how the space between your ribs is like an accordion stretching and opening. If the horse is walking, let the his movements deepen the stretch. Breathe in and out in rhythm with the stride, unlocking any tight areas. Breathe out the tension and stress of the day and breathe in the wonderful, relaxed feeling of connecting with your horse, slowing down, and being present.

Open at the hip, do not hollow your back.

STEP 2:

Reach back and rub the horse's hindquarters. Be sure not to surprise him when you do. Gradually, rub your way farther and farther back, deepening the stretch and allowing the waves of the walk to pass through your body. Allow the front of your body to open and lengthen as you breathe deep into your lower back and belly.

Tuck your tailbone under as if you were a frightened dog, sitting on the back of your seat-bones. Be sure not to hollow your lower back. Instead, open at the hip.

STEP 3:

Repeat on the other side.

STEP 4:

When you and your horse are relaxed and comfortable you can proceed to do it at various gaits.

Ask:

- Am I staying in the middle of the saddle?

- Am I present and in the moment, being sure to remain open and aware of all that is taking place in the here and now?

- What does my horse think of the change in my intentions?

- What do I notice is different in his body language?

- Do I have soft eyes and soft awareness?

- Am I building confidence and trust?

Visualize:

- The ribcage is like an accordion. Feel it open and close with the horse's movement and your own, allowing your ribs to expand and fold.

- Let your back be wide, full, open.

- Your lungs are like balloons; you suck air in, filling and expanding the ribcage.

For a Free Video, Coach On Your Shoulder Audio Lesson and PDF related to this particular stretch go here:

https://www.jackandpaulacurtis.com/pl/76343

EXERCISE THREE: THE WIDE AND OPEN BACK

In the following stretch, you are going to place your leg over the front of your saddle's knee rolls, or fenders. Your horse must be mellow and relaxed for you to do this, and it can be helpful if you have a handler to steady your horse and walk beside him. Begin at the halt; when you are ready and your horse is comfortable, proceed at the walk.

Summary of Steps:

- Begin at the halt and have a handler for your horse. Take your foot out of the stirrup and place a leg (later, both legs) over the front of the fender or knee roll.

- Tuck your seat under and slouch in an exaggerated way.

- Then lift your ribcage and sternum from mid-back.

- When you are comfortable you can do this at the walk.

Have an instructor or handler hold your horse. Notice the riders flat back.

THE WIDE AND OPEN BACK - THE STEPS IN DETAIL

STEP 1:

Be sure to do this at a halt with a handler initially. Beginning with one leg at a time, drop your stirrup and raise your leg, placing it over the knee roll or fender of the saddle. Tuck your seat under as much as possible, so you are sitting on the back of your seat bones. Sometimes it is necessary to lift the seat off the saddle, tuck it under and then sit back down.

Place your hand on your back and feel how it is very wide, full, and open. If you are comfortable, and your horse is okay, go for a walk with your leg placed like this. Again, a handler can be very helpful. When you feel confident, you may place both legs over the front of the saddle or you may continue with the exercise, one leg at a time.

STEP 2:

Now get really slouchy all the way from your head and neck down to your seat. Think of opening all of the little spaces between the dorsal—the back or posterior—side of each vertebra and rib. Let the movement of your horse's walk gently rock your back, stretching it fully.

STEP 3:

Breathe deeply into the stretch and allow yourself the time to explore. Then, slowly lift your sternum and rib-cage, while keeping your leg (or legs) over the front of the saddle. Stretch as tall as you can in this position. Pretend there is a bungee cord attached to your sternum, lifting and elevating it straight up toward the sky. Breathe fully into your lungs, filling both your lower back and chest, creating a wide expanse throughout your torso. Feel your pelvis dropping deep into the saddle.

Slowly, bring your leg (or legs) down while keeping your open chest and deep seat. Find a neutral seat and enjoy the new body feel you have discovered. Sometimes I find closing my eyes can be very helpful as I explore the new sensations in my body. But safety first! You may want to limit the time you spend with your eyes closed, however trustworthy your horse, or you should ask someone to walk by your side.

Ask:

- How does my breathing change from the beginning to the end of this exercise?

- Does my chest and lungs feel more expansive?

- How does my seat and back move differently with the horse's walk?

- Do I feel any difference in my horse's way of going?

- Did my horse's expression change in any way? If so how?

Visualize:

- A bungee cord is attached to your sternum, pulling it upwards toward the sky.

- Your front side and back side form parallel lines of equal length.

- Your low and mid-back are a wide and open expanse.

When you can flex and stretch your back, it allows you to both feel how much range you have, as well as increase the range available to you. A soft flexible back allows you to go with your horse's movement, absorb shock, and remain comfortable as you ride. Remember that pain is a warning. If it hurts, modify the stretch, do not stretch as far, or save the exercise for later.

EXERCISE FOUR: EXPLORING THE BACK'S FULL RANGE

Summary of Steps:

- At the walk assume the jumping position. As an option, you can remain seated.

- Hunch/round your back like a cat or tuck your "tail" between your legs like a scared dog, as you touch your chin to your chest.

- Hollow your back; lift your chest and chin, pushing your "tail" out behind you.

- When you are comfortable, this can be done at the trot and canter.

EXPLORING THE BACK'S FULL RANGE - THE STEPS IN DETAIL

Step 1:

Assume a jumping position or two point position. This is a position in which you are standing slightly in your stirrups, while folding at the hip. (about 30 degrees or so) If you are in a western saddle, that is fine. Just be careful of the horn! The exercise can be done seated as well.

Step 2.

Begin by arching your back like a cat. (A rounded or hunched position.) Open all of the spaces between your ribs along the back of your body. Begin with your bottom rib and then move your way upwards allowing the horse's movement to coax the little muscles between your ribs to let go and open. Breathe deeply into the back to increase this stretch. Drop your chin to your chest and let your head hang. Tuck your tail under like a dog further increasing the stretch along your backside.

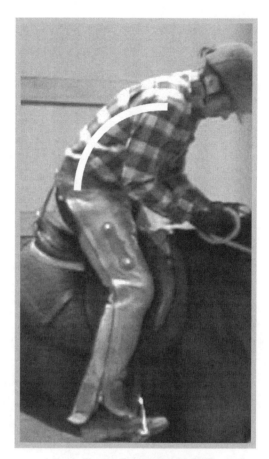

Rounding or hunching the back.

Step 3.

Next, you are going to hollow your back, opening the spaces between the ribs along the front of your body. Lift your head skywards and draw your shoulder blades together. Breathe deeply into the chest. Push your stomach out in front of you as you drop your ribs both down (at the bottom of the ribcage) and lift up (at the top of the ribcage).

You are going to move between arching and hollowing your back, slowly and purposefully as you allow the horse to move you. This exercise can be done at a trot and canter when you are comfortable.

Notice your breathing.

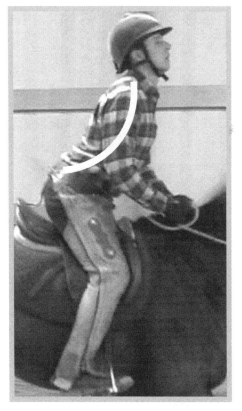

Hollowing the back.

Ask

- Where does the breath reside when I am in a hollow position versus a hunched position?

- Is one position easier than the other?

- When I hunch can I feel as though I drop my sacrum toward the saddle, draw my chin toward my chest lengthening the entirety of my back?

- When I hollow my back am I lifting my head and sternum upwards toward the sky? How does it feel?

Visualize

- You have an accordion ribcage, all the spaces between the ribs open and close as the horse's movement passes through them.

- You are a cat arching its back when hunching.

- You are a sagging rope bridge when hollowing.

EXERCISE FIVE:
OPEN AND ALLOW THE
POSITIVE ENERGY IN

"Always approach your horse with positivity and gratitude."

We spend much of our day in a contracted state, hunched over our phones or computers. This stretch really opens us up and feels wonderful! The mind and body are very connected and changing our posture this way will bring about a change in our attitudes.

Have a handler for your horse in this stretch.

Steps

- With a handler holding your horse, drop your reins and palms up stretch your arms outward.

- Lift your chest and head (optionally closing your eyes).

- Slowly move your arms up and down finding areas that feel great.

Notice the riders open chest and upturned palms.

OPEN AND ALLOW THE POSITIVE ENERGY IN - THE STEPS IN DETAIL

Step 1

Drop your reins. (Have a handler holding your horse.) In your mind's eye, picture a Native American on his horse at the edge of a cliff. Arms outstretched, head lifted skyward.

Step 2

Lift your head and chest upward, close your eyes, and feel the uplifting energy course through your body. Feel the entire front of your body stretch, lengthen, and open. Breathe deeply into your chest, as you imagine a wind blowing at your upturned face. If at any point you need to yawn, assume a normal position, sit tall and allow the yawn to go all the way into your abdomen.

Step 3

When you do this stretch you will want to experiment with moving your arms into different positions. Lowering and raising them and finding positions that facilitate a stretch that feels wonderful.

Ask

- Do I feel uplifted?
- Do I feel energized?
- What do I notice in my horse after doing this exercise?
- How does my horse feel when I am positive and grateful?

Visualize

- You are the Native American, feeling the sun warm you as the wind blows in your face.
- You have a button-down shirt, the buttons are popping off as you stretch the front of your body.

EXERCISE SIX: SIDE BENDS

We need to receive the motion of our horse both front-to-back and side-to-side. After doing this exercise at the walk you will feel loose and limber throughout the length of your spine, with a greater range of motion laterally.

Steps

- Put your left hand on your hip keeping your right hand on the reins and create a "C" shape with your body to the left.

- Breathe into your right lung and bring your left ear toward your shoulder.

- Lift your left seat bone as you drop your right seat bone toward the saddle.

- Switch sides.

Keep even contact in both seatbones.

SIDE BENDS - THE STEPS IN DETAIL

Step 1

You can do these side bends with your hand on your hip or your arm outstretched, use both and find which facilitates the stretch that feels best. You will be making a "C" with the side of your body. As you make the "C" allow the horse's movement to help you move into the stretch, each step of the horse will entice you to stretch deeper.

Step 2

Breathe more fully into the lung on the side you are stretching. Allow your accordion lung to expand and take in air. As you breathe into your lung, allow it to push your ribs outward and upward deepening the stretch. Drop your ear toward your shoulder, increasing the stretch even farther. We are getting the cerebrospinal fluid flowing, using our breaths to help facilitate this.

Step 3

Lower your seat bone on the side you are stretching, helping to lengthen from your seat to your ear. Contract the muscles on the opposite side of the one you are stretching. While doing this you should be feeling for a loosening and limbering from your head all the way to the sacrum.

When finishing this exercise take a moment to focus on softly going along with your horse, let your breath guide you into inner stillness as your horse's movement gently rocks you keeping you present and in this moment. Notice any changes in your horse's movement and ribcage.

Ask

- What difference do I feel when I contract versus lengthen to stretch? This should increase the stretch in different ways.

- Am I sitting over the middle of my horse as I stretch, keeping my center over theirs?

- Is the horse's movement facilitating a better stretch?

Visualize

- Your lungs are like an accordion, the air expanding and contracting your ribs as you breathe.

- Make a "C" with your body.

- Your lungs are each a balloon, you are only filling one balloon, the one on the side you are stretching.

EXERCISE SEVEN: STRETCH LIFT AND TWIST

As you do this exercise you will thoroughly enjoy a light and supple feeling throughout your body both during and afterward.

Steps

- Stretch one arm straight away from your body, palm up, parallel to the ground.

- Turn through your trunk until your palm-up arm is behind you and over your horse's hindquarters.

- Rotate through your middle until your arm is over your horses' neck.

Rider twists through his torso keeping eyes and palms up.

STRETCH LIFT AND TWIST - THE STEPS IN DETAIL

Step 1

Reach your arm straight out away from your side, lengthening across your shoulder and through your entire arm until every joint has expanded all the way into the last digit of your fingers. Rotate your palm up toward the sky. Allow the horse's movement to encourage your trunk to lengthen and support your outstretched arm.

Step 2

Rotate your trunk to the left or right causing your arm to move back over your horse's hindquarters. If you had a headlight on your chest it would be pointing away from your horse at a 45-degree angle or more. Think about your pelvis as a tripod, your two seat bones, and your pubic bone comprise it. Keep the tripod pointing straight ahead as you swivel at the waist.

Step 3

Next swivel slowly through your middle until your hand is now over your horse's mane, be sure that as you are rotating, you continue to stretch your arm .away from your body lengthening it outward.

Alternate hands as you twist and turn back and forth loosening your spine and create tone through your trunk.

Remain centered and make sure you are not accidentally squeezing with your legs. Your horse will tell you if you do!

Listen to your horse, he is constantly communicating his thoughts and feelings.

Ask

- Does my horse feel softer and more interested in me as I loosen, relax and limber up?

- What side am I tighter on?

- What motions feel good, can I deepen them?

- Is my trunk supporting my outstretched arm?

- Is my arm remaining level as I do the exercise?

Visualize

- Wearing a gold medal on your chest, hold it proudly with your elevated sternum.

- Pretend you have lasers in your fingertips and you are shooting the lasers out through them.

- Think about your spine like a barbershop pole twisting one way and then the other.

EXERCISE EIGHT: PICK YOUR HORSE AN APPLE AND PUT IT IN THE BASKET

Being able to move diagonally through our bodies is an important skill. We will be practicing this movement as well as expressing our gratitude to the horse.

Steps

- Reach an extended arm diagonally and upwards, stretching across the front of your body.

- Move your arm over the top of your head tracing a rainbow arc, back to your horse's hindquarters.

- Rub your horse on the hindquarters.

Rider reaches diagonally across his body.

PICK AN APPLE AND PUT IT IN THE BASKET - THE STEPS IN DETAIL

Step 1

Begin by reaching diagonally up and across your body as though you were going to pick an apple high up in a tree. Try to keep your seat bones level in the saddle as you do so. Feel for an opening and stretching along the back of your ribcage and side as you allow your horse's walk to stretch and release you more and more with each step. As you are picking the apple, think of something you are grateful for or appreciate in your horse.

Step 2

Next, draw a rainbow arch in the air. As you draw the rainbow continue to stretch and lengthen the entire arc. Moving through this range think of breathing in deeply as you pick your apple and breathe out as you are reaching back to put it in the basket. (The basket is on the horse's rump.) This slow and purposeful breathing brings a permeating calm into your body and your mount's, allowing you to truly reward him through inner stillness.

Step 3

Do this until you can reach behind you as though there is a basket on your horse's hindquarters, stay there for a moment and rub your horse with your hand. Give him a "mental apple", a reward, showing your gratitude for all he does for you. As you rub him, continue to allow his walk to stretch and release you along the front of your body. Be sure not to hollow your lower back when reaching back, you may need to roll your seat under.

Any quality relationship requires that each party adds value to the other's life.

Ask

- Am I reaching up and lengthening the entire time I am tracing a rainbow through the air?

- Am I thinking about what I am grateful for and express it through rubbing?

- Do I notice a shift in my horse when my display your gratitude?

Visualizations

- Picking an apple.

- Tracing a rainbow arc.

- Rub your horse with your hand.

CONCLUSION

When we have a large range of motion and flexibility in our torsos, it can be extremely helpful in finding the ideal position for us. We become limber and are strong through lengthening not contracting. We become more aware of our backs and can find their neutral positions.

When we think about the things we are grateful for, and express it to our horse, itcauses us to change our energy, approach, and feel. In turn, we find our horse is a substantially more active, interested participant when approached in this way.

A SOFT HIP AND RELAXED LEG

<hr>

A soft and relaxed leg can guide and support with feel.

EXERCISE NINE: A STRETCHED AND OPEN SEAT HIP AND THIGH

<hr>

This stretch is akin to a standing quadricep stretch. It is very helpful to have a handler for your horse the first few times you do this. Begin by doing it at a standstill, and then do it at a walk. When doing this exercise be sure to read your horse's expression, and notice what he is thinking. Because you are bringing your foot to your hand your horse may be unsure of what you are doing.

This exercise is a bit of an advanced exercise in the respect that it can be uncomfortable for some to do. If you are able to do this exercise you can reap some great rewards! If not, that is okay. You will want to work on stretching your thigh and hip flexors out of the saddle, which will also be of great benefit to you.

Steps

- Bend your knee and bringing your heel towards your seat, take ahold of your foot.

- Deepen the stretch by flattening your lower back, rolling your seat under and stretching tall.

- Release your foot being sure to do it slowly as to not surprise your horse. Switch Sides.

This rider's back remains flat as she stretches her thigh.

A STRETCHED AND OPEN SEAT HIP AND THIGH – THE STEPS IN DETAIL

Step 1

Bring your foot slowly to your hand and place the toe of your boot in your hand. You will feel a stretching along the front of your thigh and into your hip. Imagine you are lengthening your thigh back and down, toward your horse's hind legs. When you are comfortable enough to do this at the walk, allow the horse's movement to stretch you with every stride.

Step 2

Be aware of your back and try not to hollow it as you perform this stretch. To deepen the stretch, flatten your back and contract the muscles of your buttocks. You may need to roll your seat under in order to help the back remain flat.

Step 3

When you release your foot be sure to do it slowly and allow the leg to settle back down softly so you do not surprise your horse. Switch sides.

Ask

- Am I careful not to hollow my back?

- Can I grow tall in my torso as I stretch down and back with my knee?

- Is my horse okay with me stretching this way?

- Where do I feel the stretch most?

Visualize

- Tuck your tailbone like a scared dog to deepen the stretch.

- Drag you knee in the arena sand allowing it to pull your leg backward.

- The frontside of your body lengthening and opening.

EXERCISE TEN: THE HIP AS A HINGE

As riders, we need to be able to isolate the hip joint and allow smooth movement to happen there. In this exercise, your balance and ability to move from the hip will grow.

Steps

- Assume the jumping position.

- Fold at the hip maintaining a flat back.

- Keeping your spine in line over your horse's spine, touch your toe.

- Practice opening and closing your hip angle alternating toe-touching hands.

Keep your stirrup leather perpendicular to the ground as you reach towards your toe.

THE HIPS AS A HINGE – THE STEPS IN DETAIL

Step 1

Stand in your stirrups with a slight bend in your knee, (similar to a jumping position). Find a good balance over your feet where you do not feel as though you need to use your horse's neck to balance. You can move your feet in different positions to facilitate this, fine-tuning the balance by moving the upper body forward and backward to keep 50 percent of your mass on either side of your vertical leg.

Step 2

Keeping your center over the middle of the saddle and your spine in line with your horse's spine, fold at your hip maintaining a flat back as you do so. Be sure to only fold at the hip, imagine your torso is a rectangle, keep your front and back equal length. Close your angle as close as you can toward your horse's neck, keeping your back flat like a table, and isolating your hip joint. As you are folding, do not tip the scale, keep half of your rectangle torso in front of your vertical leg and the other half behind. We want to maintain balance and control of our movement. You may need to move your seat slightly rearward, toward the cantle of the saddle, to keep your center over your horse's center.

**If you are falling forward be sure to take your seat

back toward the cantle as a counterbalance to your upper body moving forward. Your stirrup leathers should remain close to perpendicular to the ground with half of your mass in front of them and the other half of your mass behind them.

Step 3

To increase the difficulty and coordination, touch your toe. (It's hard to do correctly in a western saddle.) It is important when touching your toes that your spine remains in line with your horse's. Do not lean, only fold at the hip. You can also reach forward toward your horse's ears as you fold, stretching long across the top of your back.

A variation of this is to do it in a seated position and open and close the hip angle while seated. Again, practice the isolation of the hip joint.

Keep your spine over your horse's spine and you articulate at your hip.

Leaning to far over the side of the horse.

Step 4

Open your body slowly and purposefully away from your horse's neck by opening the hip angle rather than drawing your body up by hunching your back.

Watch your horse's reaction. If he is upset, you may be

gripping and squeezing with your legs to balance and he is trying to tell you.

"Horses can be great teachers if we remember to listen."

Ask

- Does my leg remain perpendicular to the ground?
- Is my back remaining flat?
- Is my spine in line with my horse's?
- Is my center remaining over my horse's center?

Visualize

- Your rectangle torso, remaining so when opening and closing.
- Your hip is a hinge, and your thigh and torso are the flat fixed plates opening and closing around that hinge.
- Feel your gliding hip joint, working as though it is a ball bearing, swiveling as you open and close the angle of your body toward and away from your horse.
- Your back remains flat like a table.
- You are a balance scale, always keeping the weight equal front and back.

EXERCISE ELEVEN: SCISSORS THE LEG TO RELEASE HIP TENSION

Being able to move the leg from the hip is an important skill when riding. Once you get good at this skill it becomes much easier to create a more effective set of seat and leg aids. At the outset make micromovements, increasing the range gradually.

Steps

- Drop your left stirrup and slowly bring your leg forward from the hip.

- Slowly and purposefully bring your leg back from the hip.

- Switch legs. Eventually, scissors both legs at the same time, one leg swings forward from the hip as the opposite leg swings back from the hip.

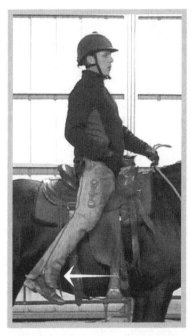

Bring leg back from the hip joint, keeping back flat.

SCISSORS THE LEG TO RELEASE HIP TENSION – THE STEPS IN DETAIL

Step 1

Drop your left stirrup. Bring your leg forward not by pushing your foot forward and straightening the knee, but by swinging it forward from the hip. Initially, it can be helpful to bend the knee slightly to assist.

Step 2

Bring your leg back from the hip. You may straighten the knee initially to help you increase the range of motion, but then see if you can keep your leg with a slight bend in the knee.

Step 3

As you get good at doing this exercise with a single leg, then try doing it by scissoring your legs, one forward and one back then switch. It is not about swinging the leg quickly, move your leg slowly and deliberately.

If your horse gets troubled offer guidance and support. Be the presence your horse goes to for help.

Scissoring both legs, one forward, one back.

Ask

- Did I start with micromovements?

- Where do I feel the tension?

- Is one leg easier to move than the other?

- How smoothly can I move my leg from one position to another?

- Am I more aware of my seat?

When doing this exercise is my horse clear on my intentions? You may need to rub him to let him know you are not asking for anything.

Visualize

- The legs are like the blades of a scissors, moving from the point that they connect at the hip.

EXERCISE TWELVE: FIND A DEEPER SEAT WITH LEG LIFTS

A deep seat allows you to sit into the saddle and feel stable and secure. One of the things that can get in the way of a deep seat is pinching with the thighs. This exercise will help you let go of that tension and feel how it allows your seat to really connect with your saddle.

Steps

- Lift your leg away from the saddle. Do not lift it very far initially.

- Move your leg forward and back lifting it in various positions.

- Switch legs and eventually alternate lifting legs within the horse's walk. There will be a time in the horses gait in which it will feel most natural to lift your leg.

Notice the daylight between the entire leg and the saddle.

FIND A DEEPER SEAT WITH LEGS LIFTS – THE STEPS IN DETAIL

Step 1

Lift one leg away from your horse's side from the hip. Initially, it can be helpful to bend the knee to assist you in making this motion. Only make small motions and then gradually build on your range of motion.

Step 2

Move your leg forward and back from the hip and explore the range of motion you find. In each position try lifting your leg away from the saddle.

Step 3

Once you feel comfortable lifting each leg independently, you can then "walk" by lifting one leg slightly out and away from the hip and then the other. Try to time it within your horse's movement.

At the end of this exercise, you should sense a deepening in your wide and open seat. Imagine the seat sits into the horse's back as well as surrounds it. The leg should now grow longer and feel like it can "hug" the barrel of the horse.

Ask

- Do I feel an increased awareness of my seat bones when doing this?

- Does it deepen and widen my seat?

- How does my horse react to me doing this?

- Am I being sure to make small movements that are not painful?

Visualize

- Your seat grows roots and anchors itself into the saddle and around the horse's back.

- When you let your leg hang it now "hugs" your horse.

EXERCISE THIRTEEN: STAND AND IMPROVE BALANCE

Awareness of your balance over the stirrups is essential. It is something we should check for regularly.

Steps

- Rise out of the saddle into a standing position over your stirrups. You may need to move the lower leg position to facilitate this.

- Sit down slowly and carefully so as not to fall down onto your horse's back. At all times, be careful not to pull on your horse's mouth.

Find a position where you are balanced over your feet.

STAND AND IMPROVE BALANCE – THE STEPS IN DETAIL

— • • — ◉ — • • —

Step 1

I recommend doing this at a standstill, before trying it in movement. Rise up out of the saddle and stand tall in your stirrups, in an upright position. Feel as though you have a rope attached to your belt pulling you forward and upwards toward the sky. You may need to make a few adjustments to your lower leg to facilitate your ability to stand up in the irons. Really stretch tall through your body, feeling as though you are lowering your feet toward the ground and your head in the clouds.

**When you have your leg under you it is very easy to rise up out of the saddle. If you find it hard to rise out of the saddle, then you may need to bring your leg back to facilitate this. If you find yourself falling forward as you rise out of the saddle, then you may need to bring your leg forward.

Step 2

Gradually lower yourself toward the saddle, settling back into it softly and quietly. Pretend you are sitting on a balloon and you do not want to pop it. Anytime we sit on our horses we want to be respectful that it is their back we sit upon. We are looking to increase control of our bodies. These exercises force you to find a balance over your feet, causing you to move your leg into a position to facilitate control when rising out of and lowering into the saddle.

**A variation of this can be at the posting trot where you stand for two beats or sit for two beats.

Ask

- Where do I need to place my lower leg, so I can do this with the least amount of effort possible?

- Am I standing tall?

- How long can I remain in this position?

- Am I balanced enough to be able to lower myself into the saddle, rather than fall back into it? (If you need to grab mane or the saddle to help assist you initially that is fine, just do not use the reins!)

- Is my horse telling me I am gripping with my legs?

- Am I holding my breath?

Visualize

- A rope attached below your belly button pulling your center over your feet. Stacking your balanced body over your feet.

- Stretch long and tall from both ends of the body, Head in the clouds, and feet in the sand.

- Careful not to pop the balloon on the saddle.

EXERCISE FOURTEEN: PLAY WITH HIP ROTATION

In this exercise, you will find a connected thigh not only distributes your weight effectively over the horse's ribcage but is also able to clearly communicate to the shoulder. The hip is a mobile ball and socket joint and not only can it open and close, but it can also swivel.

Steps

- Externally rotate the thigh from the hip.

- Internally rotate the thigh from the hip.

- Find the position that allows your knee and hip to point straight ahead, with good contact along the entire inner thigh and knee to the saddle.

PLAY WITH HIP ROTATION – THE STEPS IN DETAIL

Step 1

Begin with pointing your knee away from your saddle, externally rotating your leg from the hip joint. Open and stretch the inner part of your thigh. You will feel the back of your thigh touching the saddle or there may be no contact with the saddle. You will notice the lower leg and heel come into contact with your horse's side as your toe and knee point outward. You may feel your seat pinch the saddle.

External rotation of hip.

Step 2

Next, internally rotate from the hip, so that knee points inward toward the saddle as your heel and lower leg move away from the horse's ribcage. This time you should feel your thigh connect with the saddle. You will feel a stretch along the outer part of your thigh and into your buttock.

Internal rotation of hip.

Step 3

Move between internal and external rotation, hold each position and notice how the horse's movement passes through your body, while you are aware of your contact points along your leg, in your seat, etc.

You're looking to find a position where you have the contact along the entire inner thigh but still are able to allow the horse's movement to pass through with a mobile soft hip, seat, and back. You do not want to be gripping or pinching with your thigh or knee.

Ride your horse in a way that distributes your weight over the horse's ribcage, not just the top of his back. Notice how a degree of internal rotation helps facilitate that. In this position, we can communicate clearly to our horse, by just a tightening of the muscles in our thigh.

Always be sure to take into consideration your horse's input on any given position.

Ask

- Which movement is easier for me?

- How does it affect my lower back?

- How easily can I move from internal to external rotation?

- Does my horse appreciate me riding on my thigh rather than my seat alone?

- Where do I feel connection points of the leg against the saddle?

Visualize

- Your femur connected to the ball head at the top of it, imagine what is happening to the ball in the socket as you move your femur.

- Visualize the swiveling movement of the ball in the socket as you internally and externally rotate.

- Heel pointing 90 degrees away from the horse or toward the horse, all from the ball and socket.

When you use your leg aids do not forget what an important tool the thigh is! You can position the shoulders and withers by just contracting the thigh on one side or another.

EXERCISE FIFTEEN: KNEE BENDS

Get the juices flowing! The knee is part of our suspension system, along with our hip, ankle, and back to some extent. It is essential it is well oiled, loose, supple and flexible. Let this exercise "get the juices flowing" to enable your knee to do its job.

Steps

- Take your feet out of the stirrups, straighten and stretch your legs.

- Move your leg forward and back stretching it in each position.

- Bend your knee, again moving your leg forward and back. Then shake it out and let your leg hang heavy and long.

KNEE BENDS – THE STEPS IN DETAIL

Step 1

Take your foot out of the stirrup. Straighten your leg and stretch it straight down toward the ground, really lengthening it. Imagine your leg is growing from your hip down toward the ground.

Let the leg hang long from the hip and knee.

Step 2

Stretch the leg straight down toward the ground, out in front of you, and behind you, allowing the stretch to move through the length of your leg and into your hip. You can even make little circles with your leg, finding areas that feel good and stretching into them. Do this both with your knee bent and your leg straight.

Bend the knee as you move through the range of motion.

Step 3

Bend your knee as far as you can and straighten and stretch it to its fullest, expanding the space in your knee. Move your leg forward and back as you are doing this Be aware of any tight areas and work them loose. Shake it out! Drop your leg long toward the ground and shake it out! Let it hang and grow heavy allowing the horse's movement to lengthen, stretch and in general help you grow the feeling of a long, heavy leg.

Along with the hip and ankle, the knee forms the lower part of our "suspension system." It allows us to absorb shock, and receive the horse's motion, allowing them to move well underneath us. Keep your springy, soft knee throughout the rest of your ride.

Ask

- At the beginning of the ride how does my leg feel?

- Am I pushing on my stirrups?

- Is there tension in my back, buttocks, and hip?

- What changes do I feel after doing this exercise?

- Does my leg feel longer and heavier?

- Does my horse need help relaxing and understanding why I am moving my leg?

Visualize

- Imagine a well-lubricated knee joint as you do this, keeping the motion smooth.

- A little spring in the knee, opening, and closing.

Does your horse understand your intentions? How can you be clearer in your communications so they do? Sometimes it takes a kind word or a rub.

EXERCISE SIXTEEN: HAPPY FEET AND LOWER LEG

A soft flexible, mobile leg means the whole leg, from hip to toes, should possess the qualities of being soft and flexible. Let's make sure we have that!

Steps

- Drop your stirrup, trace a circle in the air with your toes, start small and work bigger.

- Write the alphabet in cursive with your toes.

- Do steps 1 and 2 and alternate between curling your toes and spreading them.

- Play the piano with your toes.

HAPPY FEET AND LOWER LEG - THE STEPS IN DETAIL

Step 1

Drop your stirrups, move your ankle through a range of motion by tracing a large purposeful "O" in both directions with your toes. Let the leg hang heavy and long as you do this exercise, breathe deeply allowing the stretch to really sink into the long heavy relaxed leg. Really explore the range of motion of the ankle, and stretch the toe straight down at the bottom of your "O" and straight up at the top of it.

Step 2

Now try writing the alphabet in cursive with your toes. Get your ankle gliding smoothly, staying in areas that are tight to work out kinks. You may feel tension up your leg and into your calf.

Step 3

Experiment gripping the toes as though you are picking up a pencil off the floor with them. Continue to write the alphabet and circle the ankle. Notice how gripping the toes causes immobility clear up to the hip. Some things as small as your toes can affect the tone and flexibility of the entire leg.

Step 4

Play the piano with your toes, and spread them apart, how does this feel and change your range of motion? Continue to write the alphabet, it should feel better. Many riders inadvertently clench their toes, restricting the movement in their ankles, locking up their knees and hips.

**Pick up your stirrups afterward and be sure you keep the long, heavy relaxed leg.

Tap your feet up and down in the stirrups to make sure you are not pushing on your irons. Just let the weight of your leg be in the stirrup, no more, no less. Your ankle is part of your "suspension" system, keep it loose and relaxed once you have picked up your stirrups.

Ask

- What changes did I feel when spreading my toes versus gripping them?

- What was I most aware of?

- Am I making observations and comparisons?

Visualize

- Picking a pencil off the floor with your toes.

- Playing the piano with your toes.

- A small soft spring in the ankle absorbing shock up and down.

- Your tap dancing feet in the stirrups.

A SUPPLE RELAXED SHOULDER AND ARM

Our hand through the reins connects to a delicate place of the horse's body, in order to convey our ideas with feel and sensitivity we must be relaxed from the hand to the shoulder.

EXERCISE SEVENTEEN
REACH FOR THE CLOUDS

Open and stretch the entire arm clear to your fingertips!

Steps

- Raise your hand straight above your head, stretching tall.

- Lengthen the entire arm, to the fingertips.

- Switch hands.

Stretch from seat to fingertips.

REACH FOR THE CLOUDS – THE STEPS IN DETAIL

Step 1

Raise your hand straight above your head, stretch tall, and lengthen through the side of your body. As you reach, allow the horse's movement to loosen and move you into a deeper stretch. As you reach above your head, notice any tight areas and breathe into them releasing the tension as you breathe out. Think of your horses' movement like a wave, allow the waves to pass through you, allow them to travel up your back and out the top of your head.

Step 2

Grow your fingers upwards feeling them stretch and lengthen the tendons in your forearm. The stretching fingers pull clear to your shoulder and down your entire side. Be like a sapling growing in a forest, stretching for the sun straight and tall. You allow the wind from all directions to move you, you are supple, yet stretching and strong.

Feel your inner skin, your facia, become more and more elastic as each step of the horse stretches you and releases you like a rubber band stretching and then going back to normal. Reach down with your seat as you reach up with your hand to maximize the stretch through your entire body. In order to have a relaxed shoulder, we must have a strong, supple back for it to sit upon.

Step 3

Rub your horse when you switch hands and check how he is feeling. Notice changes in your horse's facial expression, his eyes, his mouth.

Ask

- As I open and release the upper body and my shoulder, does my hip feel more relaxed and open?

- Does my horse blow out, lick and chew, lower his head?

- Do I feel stronger and more solid as I stretch?

- Am I making observations and comparisons?

- Do I feel a difference in the happiness and joy in both myself and my horse in the rest of my ride?

Visualize

- Reaching for a cloud or a star.

- A sapling in the woods stretching for the sun, supple, strong, resilient.

- The horse's movement stretching your facia like a rubber band.

EXERCISE EIGHTEEN : A GREASED AND GLIDING SHOULDER

After this exercise, your smoothly gliding shoulder will feel great to both you and your horse.

Steps

- Begin performing a backstroke motion by stretching your arm straight in front of you with your thumb up, slowly bring it straight above your head.

- When your arm is straight above your head, turn your hand so your palm faces outwards.

- Continue the backstroke motion slowly in this way.

A GREASED AND GLIDING SHOULDER – THE STEPS IN DETAIL

Step 1

Stretch your arm straight in front of you with your thumb facing upward, slowly bringing it forward and up. Breathe in when you are moving the arm forward and upwards.

Lead with your thumb up.

Step 2

At the uppermost portion of your stroke flick your wrist so your palm faces out. Then bring your arm behind you and back to its original position. Breathe out as your arm moves back and down.

Palm out at the top of your stroke.

Step 3

Repeat the backstroke in this way slowly and deliberately taking your arm through a range of motion doing the backstroke. As you are moving your arm forward and upwards be sure to lead with your thumb, turning your palm out at the top of the stroke.

Grease the ball and socket joint of your shoulder as you work it through a range of motion. Feel for any tight or sticky areas and stay there experimenting with different ways of moving through that area so that it begins to feel smooth and gliding.

When doing this exercise try to breathe in as you are lifting your arm and out as you are lowering it.

End rotation with underhand throw.

Ask

- Am I stretching and lengthening through my torso as I do this?

- How does it feel in the rest of my body?

- How is my breathing?

Visualize

- Swimming in a pool doing the backstroke, arms effortlessly gliding through the water.

- A plane's propeller moving through its motion.

EXERCISE NINETEEN: SHRUG IT OFF!

Having a soft relaxed shoulder is essential to having a soft connection to the bit.

Tension in the shoulder area is very common. Many people hold their stress there. Let's shrug it off!

Steps

- Shrug shoulders up to ears.

- Move them in a half-circle back and down.

- Move them in a circle.

- Alternately pedal your shoulders.

SHRUG IT OFF –
THE STEPS IN DETAIL

Step 1

Shrug your shoulder up to your ears. Hold them here with tight muscles until they really want to let go. Quite often it can be helpful to overly contract a muscle that has tension so that it really wants to let go when you ask it to. Notice, what does your horse think of it? This would probably be his response to tell you when your shoulder is tight. Now that you are more aware, and are listening to your horse, you will be able to make a change if he tells you it is tight.

Step 2

Roll your shoulders back and let them settle down along your ribs. Feel for the shoulders' "home", a place where the ribcage supports them. With the shoulders here, pretend as though you are going to put them in the opposite pants' pocket.

Step 3

Alternately pedal your shoulders both forward and backward loosening and relaxing all the little muscles in the shoulder girdle. Let the movement rock you, both down into your ribcage and low back as well as up into your neck and head. Be sure your reins are long enough that you are not disturbing your horse. Let go and loosen up!

Ask

• Are there any motions that feel stuck or limited?

• Do I feel the interconnectedness throughout the entire body?

• What shoulder feels tighter than the other?

• Do they become more fluid as I move them?

• Do I feel a loosening clear up to your neck and into the base of my skull?

Visualize

• Little bike pedals attached to your shoulders pedaling them both forward and back.

EXERCISE TWENTY: CIRCLE FOR STABILITY

When we are stable, we are quiet, allowing our horses to hear our slightest whisper.

Here you will feel how the idea of lengthening can create strength and stability.

Steps

- Stretch your arm straight out and away from you, keeping it parallel to the ground.

- Feel the "corset" your torso makes as you trace circles in the air with your fingertips.

- Gradually spiral in and out as you lengthen clear out through your fingertips. Switch hands.

Keep arm straight, and eyes up.

CIRCLE FOR STABILITY –
THE STEPS IN DETAIL

Step 1

Stretch your arm straight out to the side, remaining parallel to the ground. Stretch clear through your fingertips.

Step 2

Be aware what needs to occur in your torso and abdomen as the muscles create tone, and lengthen to help support your arm. Notice how this is a very limber type of stability allowing your horse to move freely underneath you. Feel the quietening of the whole body as it supports the outstretched arm.

Step 3

Begin drawing a circle in the air with your fingertips, starting small, and then getting larger. Be aware of the difference in your muscle tone as you move through this range of movement.

Lengthening is a concept that brings about strength in a way that facilitates good mechanics. It makes one freer, stronger and more resilient. You will feel strength created in your torso as you lengthen your arm away from you. The strong torso still allows freedom of movement without restriction. When you are feeling a lack of strength in your trunk, reflect back on this exercise, and even do it for a moment or two to regain the tone you are looking for.

Ask

- Am I allowing arm to really stretch as I am tracing the circles?

- Can I keep my arm moving smoothly through the motions? Find places that feel choppy and remain there experimenting with lengthening and relaxing until they loosen up.

- Do I feel a quietening in my body, as it steadies, and carries my outstretched arm?

Visualize

- The spaces in all of your arms joints opening clear to your fingertips.

- Your solid middle is like that of an oak tree, growing tall and strong out of its roots in the saddle, supporting its limbs.

EXERCISE TWENTY-ONE: STRIKE A POSE

When we are told to sit up and put our shoulders back, oftentimes we hollow our lower back to achieve the "look" of getting the shoulders back. This exercise helps lift and open the ribcage and isolate the shoulder blade to correctly bring your shoulders back.

Steps

- Put your hand behind your helmet.

- Stretch your elbow back behind you.

- Bring the elbow forward and back increasing the stretch.

Elevate sternum as you move elbow back.

STRIKE A POSE –
THE STEPS IN DETAIL

Step 1

Place one hand behind your helmet, be sure to not let your hand push your head forward.

Step 2

Stretch your elbow behind your head allowing your shoulder blade to glide along your rib cage back, down, and toward your spine. Open and lift your chest, while keeping the lower back soft and neutral, as you stretch the elbow back. Expand the ribcage, as you anchor the shoulder blade into it. Pretend as though you are taking your shoulder blade and trying to put it in a back pants' pocket on the opposite side of your body.

Step 3

Move the elbow forward and back slowly. Feel the movement of the shoulder blade against your ribcage as it slides along the ribs. Increase the stretch each time you bring your elbow behind your head, feeling as though you are tucking your shoulder blade into the opposite back pants' pocket. Keep your head over your shoulders as you do this.

Ask

- Can I feel my shoulder blade gliding and moving smoothly across the ribcage?

- Is one side easier than the other? Can I keep my "anchored" shoulder blade in place as I lower my arm and hold my reins?

- Do I feel as though my shoulder blades have a "home" or a place to settle?

- Is one side easier than the other?

- Am I keeping my head tall?

Visualize

- As you strike your pose, pretend you have a medal on your chest and you are showing it off.

- Tying a string to your shoulder blade and to your ribcage holding it in place.

- Tuck your shoulder blade down and into your opposite rear pants' pocket.

The Accident Continued

After the accident, I was determined, and I had goals. I was going to pick up my son and daughter, I was going to ride horses again, I was going to mountain bike race again. A couple months after my shoulder surgery, I was gingerly doing these things. Breathing deeply was still painful, and it was hard to have my hands down on the bike handlebars for more than five minutes, but I was getting there.

What surprised me most was that I had some fear when riding horses. I was not expecting this. I had holding patterns in my body from the injuries, and when riding I would sometimes come up against one of these areas and it would trigger a fear response. This is where I learned how much stretching while riding can help with fear. Each ride I made sure to incorporate stretching to loosen up and work through these areas. This really helped to lessen the trigger when I rode.

I also found it fascinating how the body holds on to these experiences without us realizing. To this day sometimes when I am riding our all-terrain vehicle (which is what I rode back to the barn immediately after the accident) and it hits a bump just so, I immediately feel fear rise up in me as my body braces. It is almost unbelievable to me the mind and body connection, right on down to the cellular level. While I write this, I am thinking maybe I should try doing a few stretches on the ATV!

The stretching helped me find my new functional position, and work through my fear. It also helped me to breathe deeper, as this was something I was still working on.

After a while, I was comfortable riding, but when jumping there was still fear. My core was not as strong as it once was, and I could not place my hands down on the horse's neck because my fused wrist and arthritic fingers on my left, and my right shoulder was still too weak. I needed to get over my fear and strengthen my core. Luckily, we had an indoor mountain bike park locally and I started going there mid-winter. They had progressive lines incorporating jumps, ladder bridges, and balance beams to ride your bike over. It was scary, and challenging, and fun. My breathing got better, my core and shoulder strength was beginning to return and my "fear muscle" was getting worked.

This sort of activity helped me learn to incorporate something a bit scary regularly into my life to keep my fear muscle strong. The more you work this "muscle" the more you prove to yourself that you can work through scary situations and succeed. It is only fair to the horse to work on this off the horse as well as on.

By the time summer rolled around I was so much better. I raced mountain bikes doing quite well, and by the end of summer, just over a year after my accident I raced my first professional level mountain bike race and placed third. If not for the accident, I may not have set such high goals and pushed myself that far. Sometimes going through tough times brings out pieces of you that you did not even know existed.

Because of my arthritis, and all the surgeries I have had for both my arthritis and injuries I have learned so much about the capacities of the human body.

I have experienced the art of learning about oneself through movement, experimentation, breathing etc. The results have been profound mentally, emotionally and spiritually.

I share my experience because I know that we all have hurdles, and if I can overcome the hurdles in my life you can overcome your own. My hope is that through this book you will find tools to work through some of your physical hurdles.

THE HEAD AND NECK

※

Be sure your eyes are soft, taking in all that your horse is.

Head and neck mobility is an important thing to have and in this chapter, we are going to find a way to hold our head.

EXERCISE TWENTY-TWO: LEFT RIGHT LEFT

When crossing the street, we have all learned since being little to look in both directions. In this exercise, we are going to stretch our neck by looking left and right.

Steps

- Look over your left shoulder let horse's movement bob your head loose.

- Look over your right shoulder.

- Look left and right, making a figure eight with your head

LEFT RIGHT LEFT –
THE STEPS IN DETAIL

Step 1

To begin, look over your left shoulder while remaining straight in the rest of your body, notice how far you can move your head to the left. Be aware of how far behind you, you are able to see on this side. Then try an experiment, put your tongue in your right cheek and see if you are able to look any further to the left.

Let your head be like a bobber in the water allowing the undulating walk to bob your head loosening it even further. Repeat by looking over your right shoulder.

Step 2

Repeat looking right.

Step 3

Then move your head back and forth between the left and right loosening all of the muscles and joints of the head, neck, and shoulder. Make a figure eight with your head as you are doing this.

Ask

- How far can I see?

- Where do I feel tension/strain?

- Does putting my tongue in the opposite cheek help?

Visualize

- Allow the horse's movement to move your head like a bobber on water.

EXERCISE TWENY-THREE: HEAD CIRCLES

By the end of this exercise, your head will feel very light and airy.

Steps

- Bring your right ear toward your shoulder, switch sides.

- Roll your head in a circle, switch directions.

- Float" your head, balancing it on your spine.

HEAD CIRCLES – THE STEPS IN DETAIL

Step 1

Begin with bringing your ear toward your shoulder. Allow the horse's locomotion to help increase the stretch. To amplify the stretch experiment by; lengthening and elevating the side you are stretching on and bringing your head forward and back as you are bringing your ear to your shoulder. Switch sides. Take note of which side you feel more tension.

Step 2

Gradually roll your head in a circle left and right, chin down, then ear to left shoulder, then chin up, then ear to left shoulder, then chin down. Allow the horse's movement to assist into deepening the stretch. If you find particularly tight areas stay there for a moment and breathe into it. Switch directions.

Step 3

Once you have completed the stretch try floating your head above the body finding the spot where it is right over the top of your spine, balanced and weightless. Imagine a person with a basketball on the tip of their finger, balancing it just so.

Ask

- Can I circle my head evenly in both directions?

- How easily can I float my head over my spine?

Visualize

- Basketball balanced on a finger.

- Head filled with helium, light and airy.

EXERCISE TWENTY-FOUR: CHIN TUCKS

You will feel lengthened in the neck and upper back after doing this stretch.

Steps

- Tuck your chin to your neck while looking straight ahead.

- Lengthen the back of your head upwards.

- Move between your ordinary position and tucked position.

CHIN TUCKS – THE STEPS IN DETAIL

---·◦—◉—◦·---

Step 1

Tuck your chin to your neck while looking straight ahead. Let your head move backward as you do so.

Step 2

Lengthen the back of your head upwards. Allow the stretch to move into your upper back, and down along your spine. Be sure you are looking straight ahead as you do this. You will feel the back of your neck grow long and tall, as the necks curves flatten.

Step 3

Focus on deep slow purposeful breathing as you move between your ordinary head position and the tucked position finding the place that facilitates good breathing where your airway feels unrestricted. Picture in your mind's eye carrying a book around on your head, and how you would do that.

Ask

- How tall can I lengthen my spine as I tuck my chin?

- What changes do I feel along the length of my spine into my tailbone?

Visualize

- Carrying a book on your head.

- A rope attached to your last vertebrae pulling you upwards, creating traction along the entirety of the spine from sacrum to head.

FINDING YOUR BEST POSITION

Experimentation allows you to find what works best for you and your horse.

I did not get into the ideal position until the very end of the book because I wanted to keep your mind and body available to options. The brain and body are so plastic, but sometimes in order for them to be plastic, we need to "break the mold". When you bring curiosity (which is why I used questioning so much) into the learning process, you create unique, novel and interesting experiences. When you bring these experiences into the equation, many new neuropathways are developed, old patterns of movement are replaced with new. Guarding patterns created by old pain or injuries no longer necessary are replaced. The mind and body are removed from a contracted state and brought into a state of openness.

Then when you assume a balanced centered riding seat it becomes much easier. Your entire body is available to you. If you have done a variety of the exercises in this book, your mold should be broken, and now your body is a lump of clay for you to create the sculpture you want.

Luckily for us, we have a basic frame, our skeleton, to create the sculpture around. When we take our "framework" and line it up, each piece stacks neatly upon the other in balance. When we are in balance, it requires very little effort to maintain position and harmony. When you are in this position if your horse disappeared out from underneath you, you would find yourself standing on your feet in perfect balance.

Like we talked about in the beginning of the book, you will want to make sure your saddle is level. It is nearly impossible to find a good centered position if you are sitting on a saddle that is not level.

Camera/Video

Having a friend, trainer, spouse, or child take a short video, or picture can be extremely beneficial. You know the saying a picture is worth 1000 words. A picture can be valuable feedback to have. Most of us are carrying a phone with a camera built inside so get in the habit of using it. When you see your progress, you will be pleased.

Finding Neutral/Your Middle Position

Before we break things down into individual pieces I would like to speak to the topic of neutral. Neutral is the place I would like to be in each and every one of my joints when riding. I consider neutral to be the "middle" position. This position allows the joint to both open and close. When we are in this position it is very easy for us to follow any movement that comes our way. We relax, and riding becomes easy. Regularly ask yourself when thinking about your position, "Is XYZ in the middle of its range of motion?" If you can answer "yes" you know you are fairly close to where you should be. Sometimes it can be helpful to refer back to a stretch or two to find out what the range of that joint might be.

Your Best Seat

We are going to begin with finding our best seat. The seat is an important connection point between ourselves and the horse, and a good seat platform allows the trunk and legs to have a good place to grow out of.

Go back to the pelvic stretch where we worked on going from one extreme to the other, rocking from the front of our seat bones to the back until you can find the very middle. Remember our flashlights on our seat bones, check and be sure they are pointing straight down. When you find this middle position, you will feel the waves of the horse's movement pass through it easily and unrestricted. You may find your horse moving more freely underneath you.

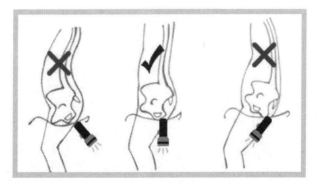

Point the flashlight on your seatbones straight down.

The neutral pelvis is the foundation for a centered balanced position. The instant you take the pelvis out of this position you throw the entire body out of balance, muscles then begin to compensate and now you are unable to freely move with your horse. When your pelvis is balanced without restriction you can effectively use it as an aid to communicate an idea to your horse. More importantly, you can stay out of your horse's way allowing them to do what you have asked them to do because you are balanced.

Your Best Trunk

When talking about the trunk I like to break it into two separate parts. I find this helps my students get the correct position.

Let's begin by starting with the low back. We want the low back to have a soft neutral curve in it. This means that it is not flattened, and not arched. To find your neutral back, alternately flatten your back and arch it, going between the extremes back and forth and then finding the middle. When you find the middle position make little movements in either direction testing to see that you have truly found neutral.

In this position, you should find a softness and widening in the low and mid back, breath into these areas allowing the breath to open this area further. The horse's movement should softly move your back, and when you place a hand on the low back each step of the walk should feel as though it moves your hand more backward than it does forward.

The abdomen carries tone, helping support the back and trunk. The tone in the abdomen is created through lengthening, not contracting. Refer back to the feeling of "the corset" in exercise #20.

Now let's talk about the mid and upper back. The spine grows out of the softly curved lower through mid-back. This helps elevate the ribcage and bring the shoulder girdle back. If you are told to get your shoulders back this would be the place I would start.

Lift the upper back from the mid-back, to elevate your ribcage and sternum. When your ribcage is lifted it gives your shoulder to have a natural place to lie. Like your lower back, your ribcage along the front of your body should feel wide, open, and soft. Breathe into the entirety of your trunk, filling the abdomen, low back, and chest. Notice the inner stillness and relaxation this brings, along with strength and tone.

The soft following hip, and strong solid torso, allow you to ride all movements without spilling a drop. All sides of your mug remain parallel to one another.

After working through this you will find that the front side of your trunk and the backside help form a rectangle, with each side being the same length. I like to picture my torso like a rectangular mug remaining fairly level so as not to spill, at all three gaits. The soft following hip forms the hinge allowing the femur/torso angle to open and close so as not to spill a drop. The handle of my mug is in line with my spine, reminding me to ride with my seat and back. My nice strong solid back sends the horse a message; lengthen, shorten, elevate, turn, stop. All from the connection of my back to my horse's back.

To communicate to your horse, use your back. (the mugs handle)

Your Best Shoulder and Arm

The shoulder girdle sits on the lifted sternum and ribcage. It is relaxed because it is stacked on a nice solid base. You want the space between your shoulders along the front of your body to be wide and open. Pretend you are tucking each shoulder blade into the opposite rear pants' pocket.

Your arm hangs down long and heavy and tired from the shoulder. You can imagine little weights in your elbows. Your shoulder and elbows are connected to your torso so that when you turn your middle, it moves your arms thereby letting the horse know where you would like him to go.

The elbow has a slight bend in it, the angle changing in relation to the horse's head carriage. The forearm has tone because when you close your fingers on the reins it creates this tone. Pretend you are holding a coffee cup in each hand, keep your hands in a position so you do not spill on his shoulder. This position will help keep your weighted elbows alongside your body.

The hand is closed softly around the reins being respectful of the horse's mouth or nose at the other end of it.

If your hand or arms get sore riding, imagine the poor horse at the other end of the reins. Try to be lighter, and explain things better, or differently.

Your Best Neck and Head

Your neck should grow tall and straight out of your upper back. With your head on top, all parts are balanced nicely upon each other.

Let your neck be like a vase sitting upon the shelf your shoulders have created. Your head is the flowers at the top.

Your Best Hip

The hip is the hinge that opens and closes the trunks relationship to the thigh. This comes from the hip, not the back. It should be soft, flexible and well-greased!

Your Best Legs

Your leg should come out of a soft hip. The femur should approximate a 45-degree angle to the ground, this keeps the hip joint in its middle range so that you are able to open and close it effectively.

Remember back to the internal/external rotation exercise, you will remember how you found a sweet spot where you found a nice even connection along the entirety of the innermost part of the thigh to the saddle. This connection then becomes a bearer of your weight, distributing it along the horse's ribcage, which invites him to lift his back into your softened seat.

Your knee should have a soft bend in it allowing your heel to come back so that it is under your hip. When you think heels down, think about lowering them toward the hind legs. DO NOT jam them down and push your leg forward, you have just worked really hard finding your best position and this simple act can ruin it!

The ankle acts as part of the suspension system, it has

a soft spring in it. In order for the spring to work keep the ankle in the middle of its range, don't bottom it out.

The toes are relaxed and comfortable. Never curling, gripping or ridged.

This is just a brief overview of a good basic position. I will need to write another book if I want to get into it fully!

Your Best You

Be present and in the moment.

Feel of and for your horse.

Be aware, with soft eyes, ears, and mind.

Breathe.

Go have fun with your horses! Go to them with gratitude, and most importantly listen to them, they are communicating to you each and every moment you are with them!

Happy Riding! Paula

For a Free Video, Coach On Your Shoulder Audio Lesson and PDF related to the stretches in this book, go here:

https://www.jackandpaulacurtis.com/pl/76343

For all inquiries, including clinic scheduling

contact Office@jackandpaulacurtis.com

For Inspiration Visit The YouTube Channel: Jack And Paula Curtis Horsemanship

HELP US OUT!

Gimli, my Appaloosa, and
I Thank You for reading this book!
I LOVE to hear what YOU have to say!
Please leave me a helpful review on Amazon and let me know
what you thought of this book.
Also, If you have a friend that may benefit from this book be
sure to share it with them!
Thank You Very Much!
Happy Riding ~ Paula Curtis

38450322R10085

Made in the USA
Lexington, KY
08 May 2019